DATE DUE

OCT.24.2001			
DEC.18.2001			
MAY 15.2002			
OCT.02.2002			
MAR 26.2003			
APR.30.2003			
SEP 17 2003			
SEP 15 2004			
JAN.05.2005			

Demco, Inc. 38-293

You
Are
What
You...

You A

e What You...

The Untied Shoelace
& Other ^revealing^ Poems

by
Alexander Jenny

illustrations by
Jenn Maynard

fumblefingers press

Publisher's Cataloging-in-Publication
(Provided by Quality Books, Inc.)

Jenny, Alexander.
   You are what you-- : The untied shoelace &
other revealing poems / written by Alexander Jenny ;
illustrated by Jenn Maynard. -- 1st ed.
   p. cm.
   Includes index.
   LCCN: 99-65451
   ISBN: 0-9674227-4-4
   SUMMARY: Humorous children's poems
on the subject of personal identity, including
"Brain-sucking monsters!" and "My on-the-
loose dream," which show that one is one's
body, brain, perceptions, etc.

   1. Identity (Psychology) in children--Humor--
Juvenile poetry. 2. Children's poetry, American.
3. Humorous poetry, American.   I. Maynard, Jenn.
II. Title.

PS3560.E535Y6 2000   811'.54
                         QBI99-1170

10 9 8 7 6 5 4 3 2 1

for our parents

...who can't take all the blame.

# of Contents

PART 1: You Are Your Body 8

PART 2: You Are Your Brain 22

PART 3: You Are How You See The World 38

PART 4: You Are How The World Sees You 96

PART 5: You Are Part Of Something Bigger 122

PART 6: You Will Be 144

Part 1

You Are Your Body
(the "you" you can touch)

IF A PEACOCK'S ITS FEATHERS
(you are your parts, partly)

If a Peacock's its feathers and Lizards are scales,
And shells are just dandy for the housing of Snails,
And Llamas are woolly, and Armadillos are neat,
Armor-plated, inflated, like a football with feet...

  Then what am I, with no warm furry coat?
  No walk-around shell? Less hair than a Goat?
  Why no Rhino-thick armor or fine feathervest?
  Are you sure this bare skin really suits me the best?

If a 'Roo is its bounce and a 'Gator its bite,
And a Bat is two wings gulping bugs in the night,
And Tigers are stripes that end in fierce claws,
And a Grizz' is unbearable fat on four paws...

    Then why is it *I* got no bear-hugging squeeze?
    No bone-crushing jaws? No spring in my knees?
    Got no stingers or suckers. Can't shock like an Eel.
    With no fangs, tusks or claws—how do *I* catch a meal?

If a Lion's a roar 'cross the whole vast savannah,
And a Monkey's a tail-hanging eat-a-banana,
And a Snake is its slither and a Worm is its wriggle,
And Hyenas are one big hysterical giggle...

    Then who am I, with no webs 'tween my toes?
    No pouch for my kiddies? No log-lifting nose?
    Can't hang by my tail to swing through the glade—
    I'm beginning to think a mistake has been made!

If a Leopard's his spots (and you know he can't change 'em),
And a Ladybug's dots, any way you arrange 'em,
And Squirrels are all squirrelly while Chippies are munks,
And Loons are just loony, and bad smells are Skunks...

    Then what sort of creature is this that I am,
    With my two scrawny legs and my skin like a ham?
    Seems to me that the others got all the best parts,
    The tusks and the claws, and the huge lion-hearts.
    Of my whole flimsy bod', just three things *I'd* retain—
    My two handy thumbs, and my very big brain.

HOW TO
EAT YOUR HAT*
*(you are what you eat:
the food chain)*

If a rat eats my hat
And Nan's cat eats that rat
And your dog eats Nan's cat
And Luke's hog eats your dog
And a cow eats Luke's hog
And I manage somehow
To chow down that cow
Well, if I can do that—
Then I'll eat my hat!

(*no hats were harmed in the making of this poem)

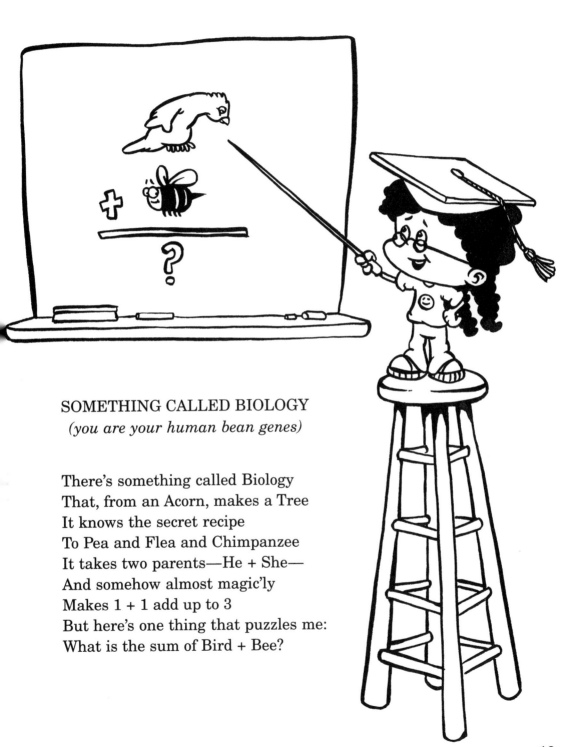

SOMETHING CALLED BIOLOGY
(you are your human bean genes)

There's something called Biology
That, from an Acorn, makes a Tree
It knows the secret recipe
To Pea and Flea and Chimpanzee
It takes two parents—He + She—
And somehow almost magic'ly
Makes 1 + 1 add up to 3
But here's one thing that puzzles me:
What is the sum of Bird + Bee?

SPECIAL DELIVERY
*(you are exactly what
your parents ordered!)*

Once upon a suppertime
(Just Mom 'n Dad 'n me)
I asked my hungry parents how
It was I came to be,
And this—a strange and juicy tale—
My father answered me:

"We wished for a pair of rosy cheeks
Like tomatoes bright and red,
And flaxen hair, like winter wheat
Sprouting from your head,
Two deep and dark mysterious eyes
Black mushrooms growing wild
To see the strange and wondrous world,
That's what we wished you, child,
And skin as soft as melted cheese
So sweet, our hearts might crumble,
A pinch of peppers, spunk & spice
For our tender little bundle,
And every wish we made, dear child,
Came true—all these and more,
The day you came into our lives—
Delivered special, to our door."

...As Father finished,
Filled his plate and
Gobbled hungrily,
I had a ghastly vision how
It was I came to be—
My parents ordered *pizza*
But the pizza guy brought *me!*

THE MARBLE AND THE PEBBLE
*(you are the nicks and scars
you collect)*

A Marble and a Pebble
Lay together in the grass
Wonderin' which of them a lad might choose,
Should one come walking past.

The Marble told the Pebble,
"You're a rough and homely thing,
So bedraggled and disheveled
With your scuffs and scrapes and dings.
Whereas I," the Marble boasted
With pure unblemished scorn,
"Am round and smooth and flawless
As the day that I was born."

"It is true," replied the Pebble,
"You are shiny, I am not.
But Marble, there's a tale to tell
For every scar I've got...

"I've rattled 'round in old tin cans,
Been nibbled on by mice,
Got homer'd off a stickball bat
And scoured by glacier ice.
I've been plunked into a puddle
And skipped across a pond
And hurled so high up in the sky
I glimpsed the Great Beyond...

"Why Marble, I've been 'et by ducks
(Always came out in the end)
And ground beneath a gravelly truck
By a ton of my best friends.
I was pecked at by a cross-eyed crow,
Got snuggled by a lovesick toad,
Been whanged and clanged down old dusty roads
Out where the high corn grows.

"So Marble, though I'm pocked and patched,
Been kicked and caromed, cracked and gashed
And whacked and thonked and
Bonked and bashed, rusted, busted,
Scored and slashed and squirrel'd away
In a chipmunk's stash,
I've earned my every chip and scratch
And wouldn't trade one single nick
For all your blank perfection—
Now stand aside, a likely lad
Comes headed our direction."

And sure enough, a passing lad
Did spy the mismatched pair...

...And carried off the *shiny* one
And left the rough one lying there,
For what do little laddies know
Of battle-scars and medals?
But now *you'll* know,
Next time you choose
The Marble or the Pebble.

BODYWORKS
(you are your bod')

Wake your body
Stretch and yawn
Drag them bones to greet the dawn!
Scratch and burp and
Fart and belch it
(You might explode if you try to squelch it)
Run the tub
Start rub-a-dubbin'
Give that grungy skin a scrubbin'
Brush those choppers
Comb those locks
Stick ten toes inside two socks
Underwear it
Pants and shirt it
(To breeze your knees, simply skirt it)
Nice and fancy, not too plain
Now go to school
And rack that brain!
Stuff one belly
Fat with yummies
(A bod' don't work on a hollow tummy)
Exercise, pump those thighs
Drawing flies?
Deodorize!
Clip some nails
And trim that mop
Time to make a potty stop
Shampoo
Rinse too
Shake it out with a boogaloo
Give a laugh
Or get it weepin'
Prop it up 'til it's ripe for sleepin'
Say your prayers
And tuck it in
Tomorrow do it all again.

MESSAGE IN A BOTTLE
(you are a link in the chain)

You're a message in a bottle
   from your parents' parents' kin,
A gift across the sea of time—
   but where'd your trip begin?

Think back, to when your pappy
   was a gleam in Grandpa's eye,
Back when that first Model-T
   went a'rolling, *you* drove by!

Long before two Brothers Wright
   eased their plane from Mother Earth,
Way back before that ol' Civil War,
   you were marching toward your birth.

Sail back before America
   when Old England ruled the waves!
Ahoy! Your message floated on,
   be it captain, crew or slave.

Through Africa or Asia
   or some sunlit tropic isle,
In every soil where humans toiled
   your roots run back a mile.

Before a wanderin' Marco Polo
   found the court of Kublai Khan
And carried home his zesty spice,
   your seed had ambled on.

Way back when Julius Caesar
  was running things in Rome
And kissin' Cleo Patria,
  you were roamin' on towards home.

Even as those old Egyptians
  built their pointy pyramids
Along the Nile, you'd been there awhile—
  why, you helped to grease the skids!

When mammoth-huntin' cave-folks
  painted pictures on their walls,
I hear *your* family portrait
  was the handsomest of all.

Back further still, when we were apes
  with a head-to-toe hairdo,
Look real close and you'll see a ghost,
  'cause kiddo, that was you.

Way back when one courageous fish
  crawled out upon dry land
And quit his gills to breathe his fill,
  you were there to shake his hand.

Back and back your message reached,
  re-shaped but never lost,
Slug or bug, your trail survived
  no matter what the cost.

Yes, even as God's lightning bolt
  touched off that bubblin' stew,
Please tip your hat, 'cause even that
  first spark of life held you!

Part 2

You Are Your Brain
(so careful what you feed it!)

BRAIN-SUCKING
MONSTERS!
(you are what you watch—
so watch out!)

"I wrote a horror story,"
Said my nutty buddy Bill,
"A scary Science Fiction Tale
To give your blood a chill
(And if it don't, I'm guessing that
No story ever will)...

"On a way-off distant planet
In a sky where stars don't twink',
The kids are plugged into machines
That tell 'em what to think.
These diabolic gadgets
Tap straight into their brains
And suck 'em out their eyeballs
Without the slightest pain.
Next, their imaginations
Are yanked out by the root,
Replaced with mashed potatoes
(Or some sugary substitute)—
Oh, woe's the kid who tangles with
A kidbrain-guzzling brute!
The kids turn dull as toadstools
And don't know *dumb* from *fun*—
They sit inside like statues,
'Stead of playing in the sun!
'Course, after that, they're zombies
With mush between their ears,

And here's the part that's spookiest:
Those kids were *volunteers*—
They all had hooked up willingly
To their fiendish puppeteers!"

"Now Bill," I said, "you stop right there!
That story's just insane!
No kid I've met would ever *let*
A gizmo gulp his brain!
So Bill, you flush that nutty tale
Straight down your nutty drain."

"I guess you're right," said nutty Bill,
"It's too farfetched to *be*."
"Of course," I said. "Now come inside,
Let's see what's on TV."
And then my nutty buddy said—

"Okay...sounds good to me."

FINDERS KEEPERS
(you are your memories—
so hold on to 'em!)

I found a tattered memory
On the sidewalk, weak and dying,
It told me YOU forgot it there
And left it, lost and crying,
But lucky me, I spotted it
As I was passerby'ing
(It glittered like a winter's morn
And smelled of flapjacks fryin')
I picked it up and fixed it up
And ATE it—now it's my'n!

SUNDAY'S CHILD

(you are your dis-position)

Monday's child makes a funny face
At Tuesday's child, a girl named Grace
Wednesday's child causes lots of woe
For Thursday's child, some kid named Moe
While Friday's child is giving and loving
And loves to give Saturday some kicking and shoving
But I'm Sunday's child, and that's the worst—
'Cause I'm littl'er than all those rats born first!

CREATURE OF HABITS
(you are a habit forming)

I've been known to crack my knuckles.
I just love to pop my gum.
I suck the creamy from the cookie
And I leave the crunchy crumb.
It's my habit, it's a hankerin'
When I hear a happy tune
To burp along in rhythm like
The toot of a bassoon.

I'm a creature of my habits—
I'm a habit-acrobat!
And the habits I inhabit
Are my natural habit-tat
Like an echo or a stutter
Loop-de-looping in refrain
Habits flit, and habits flutter,
Habits clutter up my brain!
I will say it till I'm boring
Then I'll say it twice again:
Once you've formed a nasty habit
It's a nasty ball and chain.

There are habits that are healthy.
There are habits that are wise.
There are pleasant, pleasing habits.
There are habits just my size—
Those are just the sorts of habits
It's my habit to despise!

I prefer to clean my navel
With my neighbor's garden hose,
And I like to juggle pudding
And I love to munch my toes.
It's my manner, it's my way, to
Slurp the noodles off my spoon,
And I'm fond of licking poodles in
The months of May and June.

Would you like a nasty habit,
One that grips you like a stain?
Are yours merely irritating,
Slightly grating, rather plain?
Well my friend, it bears repeating
(And repeating twice again)
Since I've formed my nasty habits
I've become a royal pain!

BILLY T. COOP
(you're not a computer...are you?!)

"The brain's a computer," hears Billy T. Coop
From his teacher one day, as she speaks to his group,
"A living machine, a PC made of goop."

"I'm not a robot!" shouts Billy T. Coop
Jumping up from his chair like a frog off a stoop
As he struggles in vain his self-worth to recoup.

"*Eyes* and *ears,* input in," teacher sweetly maintains.
"*Speak* and *shout,* output out," she further explains.
"In between is just programs—the cog-spinning of brains."

"I am *not* a robot!" cries Billy T. Coop
Now running about like a lost hula hoop
Whooping and yelling like a complete nincompoop.

"Wondrous wetware, a web of connections,"
The teacher goes on, over Bill's insurrections.
"Works perfectly well (with some small imperfections)."

"I am *not* a robot!" screams Billy T. Coop
As he spins round and round, in an infinite loop,
"I am *not,* I am *not,* I am *not,* I—"
REBOOT!

JIMMY McDEED
(you are what you read)

Hey, did you read of Jimmy McDeed?
Couldn't jump high or run races with speed,
But book after book, boy that kid could sure read.

And every last book, the last book Jimmy read
Was the book that would stick like a tick in his head,
And he'd do and he'd be what that last book had said.

Of what sorts of stuff did McDeed's books consist?
Almost too much to tell, but if you insist,
Sit yourself down and I'll read you a list:

Jim read *How-To's* and *Tell-All's* and gripping page-turners,
    Some hymn books, some slim books, some *midnight-oil burners.*
He read how *Doc Kildare* would snip, cut and sew,
    And did a head-transplant on old G.I. Joe.

He read each brand new book that came in his reach,
    Even dusty old used books for 15 cents each.
Jimmy read about *business*—the selling of things—
    And got a good price on his mom's diamond rings.

Jim read comics and diaries and *The True Crimes of Crooks,*
    Short Stories, Grand Epics, even recipe books.
He read *Fairytales Grimm* and skimmed *Goose the Mother*—
    Then he kissed one green frog and cooked up another.

Like a fresh coat of paint, a new flag up the mast,
  Each new book Jimmy read beat the pants off the last.
He read Doctor Suess and drew *Banded Bandoofles*—
  Then he read about colds and came down with the *snoofles.*

Jim read books in the library and books at the beach,
  And books in the kitchen while eating a peach.
He read old Arab tales of desert camel caravans,
  And *Kazaam!* turned his room into the Land of Endless Sands.

Jim read mysteries, Sci-Fi, biographies too—
  Why, any old book with a cover would do!
He read of crazed Ahab and *Moby* so pale,
  And in his dad's bathtub, Jimmy captured a whale.

But that *last* book! Poor Jimmy, he outdid himself—
  He read a book about *books*...

        ...now he sleeps on the shelf!

MYST'RIOUS
ICEBERG
(you are what's
hidden inside)

Myst'rious Iceberg
Up there in my head
Tips itself over
When I go to bed
And all that was hidden
Wells up from the Deep
Spillin' into my nightmares
While my body's asleep—
Every long-buried longing
And half-forgot fear
Comes a'rush to the surface
As that *brain-berg* draws near
And I twitch and I fidget,
Too sleep-froze to scream
As that huge, hairy iceberg
Starts shipwreckin' my dream...

(In the mirror, by the daylight,
There's only the tip—the *me* I can see—
And *I* captain my ship. But at night,
When the moon's right, and that 'berg makes a flip...)

...Then that submarine mountain—that *me* that's not showing—
Starts spewing its secrets as the Sandman starts snowing,
And I think to myself, *"Kid, you better get rowing!"*
Then I look out a'tremble from my dream-window perch
As I crash with that iceberg and I stop with a lurch...

...And it floats all around me, this murky *mind-junk*
That I'd locked in my attic in an overstuffed trunk:

All my dreams in the making—every *hope-beyond-hope,*
Lots of old birthday wishes,
One soap-on-a-rope,
The ghouls from my closet and under my bed,
Some *bump-in-the-night* sounds,
Some worries,
Some dread,
Old waterlogged brainstorms
And discarded notions,
Ancient *heartaches* and *grudges* and *mixed-up emotions,*
Washin' up on the tide of my restless brain-ocean...
All the words I'd misplaced on the tip of my tongue,
Every dumb TV jingle I'd ever sung,
The hot smelly breath of a fairytale dragon,
One lost babytooth,
And a little red wagon,
A swat on my butt from the day I was born,
The soft, distant *toot* of old Gabriel's horn,
A pink wilty flower from my pet Toadie's grave,
One *wish-I-did* kiss I never quite gave,
A moldy old fib that's been gnawing my innards,
One Frankenstein's Monster,
Some forky-tongued lizards,
A half-eaten sandwich,
Two bronzed baby shoes...

...And I drift through this wreckage
Still lookin' for clues
To this *me* I can't see, so far down within—

SOAP

...When that big, frosty mountain starts sinkin' again!

With a titanic *sploosh,* that 'berg dives for the deep
(As my captain—my *small I*—starts to wake from our sleep)
But before it submerges, I ask that 'berg, "*Why?*
Why, Self—I wonder—is a mind so darn shy?
Ninety-nine percent hid from its owner (that's *me!*)
Oh iceberg, *please* tell me, 'fore you slip 'neath the sea!"

...And that *me*-berg *says* something! Then it sinks 'neath a wave,
And I've chewed quite a bit on the answer it gave:

"You'd best," said that iceberg, "let a sleeping mind lie.
You can't know your *whole* self—you'll go nuts if you try!
Your *brain-gears*'d gunk up! Your tummy would churn!
Your *soul-springs* would *sproing* and your *mind-fuse* would burn!
There's too much to juggle, all this *me* inside *you*—
I'm too big," said the 'berg, "so here's what you do:

"Wake up—and *forget* me!—and have a fine day!
But come back this evening (I won't melt away),
I'll rise up when you need me—
We're bound to collide...

"...But 'til then," said the iceberg,
"I'll wait hidden, inside."

Part 3

You Are How You See The World
(this is a *big* part!)

THE UNTIED SHOELACE
(you are your work & your tools)

Today's the worst day that I ever did see,
'Cause my shoelace untied and I'm only just three
And can't tie it myself, so I walked through my town
In search a friend who might lace it back down,
'Cause an untidy lace makes an unhappy shoe,
But I hope what *I* found doesn't happen to *you*.

I first met a CARPENTER working with wood,
And asked would he help me, and he said he could.
"We carpenters like to construct things that last,
So it's best to make sure all the pieces hold fast..."
And *bam!* just like that, gave his hammer a pound
And I looked down to see my lace nailed to the ground.

I flushed out a PLUMBER and waggled my shoe—
He drew up some blueprints to show what *he'd* do.
"What you need is a system that won't fall apart.
I've some nice copper pipe we can use, for a start.
And with hot water in it, if we do it just right,
It'll keep your toes warm on a cold winter's night."

A skilled ELECTRICIAN inspected my shoe.
She hooked up some wires and ran *energy* through.
"You've a loose lace connection," she said, her face sour.
"This *heel* is not sparking. This *toe* has no power.
This shoe has gone dead, its current is nil—
Are you sure that you paid your 'lectricity bill?"

A WIZ AT COMPUTERS looked up from his work
When I showed him my shoe, gave my loose lace a jerk.
"Your problem is knotty," the computer wiz said,
"But this chip-brain can lick any riddle it's fed.
We'll create clever programs, a software attack,
But first you must tell me—are you PC or Mac?"

I next met a PAINTER, a creator of art,
And showed him my shoe, could he fix the lace part?
He studied the shoe with its too-loosy lace.
He looked from all angles, made a scowl on his face.
He scrunched up his will, took ahold of my shoe—
Then he picked up his brush and he painted it blue.

I bothered a BAKER baking sweets in his shop
To ask, could he please make my lace-flopping stop?
"My shoes have no lace, I can't help you tie yours.
But you're welcome," he said, "to a treat from my drawers.
Here's a nice toasty nibble of a cinnamon bun.
It'll make you feel better, why don't you have one?"
(And I must say it did.)

A MATHEMATICIAN considered my shoe
Till his blackboard was filled from the scribbles he drew.
"Eureka! I see why your lace is undone—
There's one end that's *longer*, plus one *shorter* one!
This problem," he said, "is quite problematical."
Then he went off to write a long proof mathematical.

MORE...

49

I next met a SALESMAN selling wares on the street
And asked "Could you help with my untied-shoes feet?"
He thought not a second. To this chap it was clear
As he calmly assured me the answer was near.
He promised to help me, the solution to choose—
"The problem," he told me, "is, you need new shoes!"

A DOCTOR passed by, in her white doctor's gown,
The very best Doc in the whole doggone town.
She examined me closely with her cold stethoscope.
Took a peek in my ear. Gave my kneecap a poke.
Then shook her head gravely, said "Poor lad, you're ill—
You've got *untied-shoe-itis!* You're in need of a pill!"

A LAWYER rushed up, interrupting my walk,
And made my head spin with his fast legal talk:
"Have you tripped? Have you tumbled? You sure you're okay?
Dear boy please be careful, please lie down right away!
We'll get *nolo contend're, heretofore, irrespective!*
We must *sue* the shoemaker, for his shoes are defective!"

I found a POLICEMAN directing car traffic.
When I showed him my shoe, his response was quite graphic:
"Who untied your lace? What did he look like?
Was he tall? Was he short? Was he riding a bike?
We'll find the ringleader! We'll catch the big cheese!"
He raced off, sirens wailing. My lace flapped in the breeze.

I met a PHILOSOPHER worldly and wise
And told him my problem. He stared in my eyes.
"Your question's an old one," came his voice deep and grand,
And he gave me an answer I did not understand:
"If your lace comes undone in a forest of green,
Is it *really* undone, if no one has seen?"

When I showed a TEACHER how my lace de-constructed,
"A textbook's your answer," the teacher instructed.
"It's one of life's lessons you must solve yourself!
To the library, child! Pull a book from the shelf!"
"I can't reach the textbooks, they're too high for me.
And I *can't* read," I said, "'cause I'm only three!"

An AUTHOR I met, a writer of books,
Read the frown on my face, and my sad, sorry looks
And said, "Sorry my boy, I can't tie your shoe,
I'm no man of action, but here's what I'll do:
I'll sit at my desk and I'll spin a great tale
Of a brave, sturdy lad whose shoelaces fail."

A stern-looking JUDGE in her flowing black robe
Tried, from her bench, my problem to probe.
She considered my case, felt the weight of my shoe—
Then decided against me, as judges may do.
"I'm 'fraid I can't help you, but my ruling is fair,
For you see, 'neath my robe, my own feet are bare!"

Then finally—at last!—I encountered Wee Bob
Who owns not one tool and works at no job,
But Wee Bob, he sat down and he tied up my shoe
So snug and so tight, like no grown-up could do,
'Cause Bob knows how shoes tie, and much more, oh much more.
See, Wee Bob is real smart—plus he's only just four.

So here is the lesson I've learned from my travels
About what to do, when your shoelace unravels:
Find a shoe-tying friend of the sort who is kind,
But still more important, has a wide-open mind.
And if the world takes the shape of the tools in *your* head,
Make sure they're good tools—or wear slippers instead.

FROM WHERE I STAND

(you are your point of view)

From where I stand (up in this tree)
You look strangely small to me.
From where I stand (down in this gully)
You're awful tall—you big old bully.
From where I stand (not in your shoes)
I can ignore you if I choose.
From where I stand (beyond this wall)
I can't see your side at all.
From where I stand (earmuffs on my head)
I can't make sense of a thing you said.
But *eye-to-eye,* here's what I see—
You look strangely just like me.

DUDLEY THE DREAMER
(you are what you dream)

Dudley the Dreamer
Had one lifelong wish,
The lone single hope his heart knew,
And here's what young Dudley
Dreamt up to do
To make his soul's yearning come true:
He wished and he dreamed,
He plotted and schemed,
He crossed all his fingers, from one to eleven,
He got on his knees and he prayed to high Heaven,
He stuck an old horseshoe inside of his pants,
He picked four-leaf clovers all covered with ants,
He paid a witch doctor to do him a dance,
He dreamed through hypnosis while under a trance,
He gazed at his navel to focus his notion,
He shaved his head bald just to prove his devotion,
He drank down a wizard's foul dream-come-true potion,
He whispered a spell and he spat in the ocean,
He quiz'd every expert and read every book
And asked those who'd done it how long it had took,
He went to bed early and stayed in bed late
The better to dream that it'd all turn out great,
But sadly neglected one last thing to do,
That *one* thing most useful
To make dreams come true—
He forgot to get up
And go *do* it.

LOOK AT ME,
I'M NUMBER THREE
(you are your place in line)

Altho' I'm just kid number three,
My parents must love me the best.
They practiced till they got it right—
Big Bro' and Sis were just a test.

They pamper me 'cause I'm the youngest.
I get away with oodles, I'm so cute.
Like putting worms in a buzzin' blender
Or dancing in my birthday suit.

Older Brother does the dishes.
Grouchy Sis cleans Tweetie's cage.
While I play, they work and grumble,
Jealous of my tender age.

But—*hey, what's this?* New baby sister?
Now *she* gets to be the pet?
Whaddya mean I gotta changer her
When she makes her diapies wet!?

They spoil her 'cause she's the youngest.
Gets away with oodles, she's so cool.
And me, I'm stuck here in the middle—
Too young to shave, too old to drool.

HAVE YOU MET
MOLLY MEANT-TO?
(you are what you do—or don't)

When I gave Molly a pretty pink sweater,
Molly meant to write a letter.

When I loaned Molly my best knapsack,
Molly meant to give it back.

When I went with my family to far-off Tibet,
Molly meant to feed my pet.
(Anybody want an upside-down goldfish?)

When I broke my arm September last,
Molly meant to sign my cast.

Now Molly wants to come to my party.
Oh, did I forget to invite you Molly?

I meant to.

I CANNOT ABIDE THE CIRCUS
(you are what you fear)

I cannot abide the circus
(I am frightened of the clown)
I have never used the bathtub
(For I fear that I might drown)
I am rightly 'fraid of fire
(And I'm none too fond of smoke)
I do not care much for eating
(For I fear that I might choke)
I am nervous in high places
(Which is why my feet go bare)
And I panic in tight spaces
(Which is why no underwear)
Tho' I have no fear of flying
(It's the crashing I abhor)
I'm in terror of that boogyman
Behind my closet door
And 'quakes and lakes and snakes and
Every uggy bug that creeps
Yes, my life's a bowl of cherries—
Just as long as I'm asleep!

PLAYING GROWN-UP
(you are what you pretend to be)

"Stop pretending!" my Pop says, all after-shave smelly
   As he puts on a suitcoat (to hide his pop-belly),
"Grow up! Pack your old *Cowboy Roy* hat away!"
   Says Pop, as he straightens his crooked toupee.

"You're too old to be playing that dumb make-believe,"
   Says my Sis, getting dressed for her date of the eve,
Painting on pretend-nails and eyelash-from-a-jar—
   "It's time you grew up! Just be who you are!"

"Yes, grow up!" says big Brother (who's short as an elf),
   Spraying stuff in his armpits, to smell less like himself.
"You're too old for tall tales," my Brother pooh-poohs
   As he sticks some height-lifters inside of his shoes.

My Mom holds her tongue, till squeezed into her girdle
   (It holds some things in, which might otherwise hurtle)
Then echoes the others while she puts on her wig:
   "No more make-believe, Son—you're getting too big!"

So now when my family says "Grow up!" and be me,
   I shake my head *yes* and pretend to agree.
I'm less troubled than eager to meet childhood's end
   'Cause I see now that grown-ups' favorite game is pretend!

A GENIUS OF FEELINGS
(you are what you feel)

Willie from Wheeling
Was a genius of feelings
And could flick his moods on like a light—
He could weep on a dime
And guffaw any time
That he wanted, anywhere, day or night.

But how strange, you might say
(And I'm quick to agree)
To *boo-hoo* when you choose
Or let loose a *tee-hee*.
It kinda reminds me what Mom used to say:
"Otis, don't make that face—
You could freeze it that way!"

Still, nothing much happened...

...Till one day, just for laughs,
Just to prove that he could,
Willie stifled a *sniffle*—he corked it up good.
He held back some teardrops,
Just to show 'em who's boss.
But you can't fool a feeling. Willie tried—

...Willie lost.

First his plumbing backed up...
Then his nerve-ends got tangled...

...And *now* look what happens when Willie's feelings
get jangled:

He pouts when he's happy!
He grins when he's glum!
Willie cries when he's cheery and sucks on his thumb!
And spiders 'n slithery snakes make him yawn,
But a bunny hops up—Willie sobs till it's gone!
If you hold Willie's hand, he gets anxious inside.
If you give him a smooch, he'll run screaming and hide!
And a stub on the toe or a bonk on the head?
Willie doesn't get pained—he gets *jolly* instead!
When a rainbow comes out, Willie's woefully sad.
If you say *"You did good, Will!"* he feels really bad.
And a *tickle's* a terror and a *pinch* is a treat,
And choc'late is horrid,
And broccoli's sweet...

And Willie's so worn out—his feelings so frazzled—
Doesn't know if he's *frizzled,* or *dizzy'd,* or *dazzled,*
But Willie knows one thing:

Don't cork up your tears!

...'Cause a too-stifled sniffle just blows out your rear.
(um, *ears*—I meant *ears!*)

NEED'A, WANNA,
GOTTA HAVE IT
(you are what you desire)

Gotta have them brand-new sneakers.
Need some tunes, and louder speakers.
Wish I might, upon a star—
A bigger bike. A faster car.
A hunky date.
The perfect wife.
The secret to Eternal Life.
(And if you're in the mood for giving,
A *horse* would make my life worth living.)
A toasty bed.
A bright nightlight.
Someone to tuck me in at night.
Success beyond my wildest dreams.
A two-pound box of caramel cremes.
Three maids to fan me while I doze.
Longer legs, and shorter toes.
(Santa, send that nifty jacket—
Can't concentrate long as I lack it.)
A hockey puck.
A fancy gown.
A long vacation out of town.
Softer hair, with brighter sheen.
A forty-nine inch TV screen.
(If there's anything you won't allow,
You might as well just kill me now.)
A cherry cone would be a treat.
Ten bucks would make my life complete.
Inner peace would make me happy—
So buy me some, and make it snappy.
A goldyfish to be my friend.
One summer that would never end.
And though I'd hate to throw a fit,
I *need'a, wanna* catcher's mitt.
And FINALLY, when I've got enough—

...A bigger house for all my stuff.

MY ON-THE-LOOSE DREAM
(you are what you dream #2)

Have you seen a lost dream come rolling by here?
   I was sleeping last night when mine fell out my ear
Then it spun down a hill and it gathered up steam,
   So please keep an eye out for my on-the-loose dream.

A dream is a wish that your heart tells your head,
   But heads can get filled up with *can't* words instead.
When some *can't do's* and *too hard's*
   Shoved my dream from my noggin,
     That dream, it whoosh'd off like one gone-goose toboggan.

Now as I pout and stare at the wall
   My dream's out carousing and having a ball,
Panning for golddust in ol' Arizony
   And riding the range on a wild spotted pony.

See, a dream is as real as most things you can touch,
   But you have to hold on or you'll lose them, 'cause such
Is the nature of dreams that they may slip away,
   'Less you feed 'em and water their roots every day.

So here I sit, with my dream-empty bean
   While my dream is out living the life of a dream
(I just got a postcard from Big Sky, Montana—
   Watch out for a dream in a bright red bandana).

Lost dreams leave a hole that burns in your belly
   Like a night without stars, or toast and no jelly.
You can cover it over, but you can't fill it in,
   Please send my dream home, so I can dream it again.

THE ACHES & PAINS
OF BAXTER Q. BLAINE
(are you what troubles you?)

Whenever I'd ask Mr. Baxter Q. Blaine,
"How are you today, Bax?" he'd lean on his cane
And he'd *grumph,* and *harumpphh...*

...Then he'd start to complain.

"How am I?"'d say Baxter. "How *am* I, you ask?
Child, even to tell you would be such a task!
Why, to list all my ills would make *God Himself* tired!
So please child, don't ask—

"But then, since you inquired..."

And as Baxter Q. listed the ailments that ailed him,
All the *sprains* and the *pains* where his bodyparts failed him
On top of the *sicklyness* that daily assailed him...

...Why, you'da thunk that a rhino or two had impaled him.

"I've got *raging lumbago,*" said poor Baxter Q.,
"The *sniffles,* a *cough,* and a *hiccup* or two,
Besides which, *one tonsil's* come down with the flu..."

I tried to console him. "Gee Bax, that's a shame—"

But B. Quibble Blaine rambled on just the same:
"...There's a *crick* in my neck, my *backbone's* a wreck,
My *knotty intestines* are shot all to heck,
I've got *rashes* and *hives* and a *too-dimpled chin,*
And my *dizzy spells* act up each time that I spin.
My *skin* is too dry and my *tears* are too wet,
And I'm sure there's a *smidge* too much *salt* in my *sweat...*"

"My that is a long list. But it's time I departed..."

"Now don't interrupt, child—I've only just started!
My *bunions* have *corns,* I got *wax* in both ears,
And a *pimple* that smarts when I sit on my rear.

My *cowlick's* unruly,
Besides, I suspect
That my *winks* are too *wrinkled*
And my *freckles* too *flecked.*
There's a *buzz* in my noggin
When I give it a nod
(And a *bug* up my nose,
Now isn't that odd?)
I've got *Tiddlywinks Elbow*
And *Badminton Thighs,*
And my eyelashes hurt
When I *bat-bat* my eyes.
There's a *frog* in my throat
And some *tadpoles* as well,
And this *bump* on my *rump*—
Did it just start to swell?"

"Well, I don't rightly know..."

"...Plus my *teeth* don't quite fit
As they should in my mouth
'Cause the *low ones* point north
And the *high ones* go south,
And my *undersides* ache
When I'm too long in bed,
And my *pants* are too short
When I stand on my head,
And it hurts much too much
When I *squat* on one knee,
And my car's leaking *oil,*
And my cat has a *flea!*"

And with that, Baxter Blaine *harumphf'd* "Have a good day!"
Then he tapped on his cane and he went on his way.
That's how things always went, when B. Q. had his say—
Wrapped up in his troubles like a bear in his fur,
Baxter tallied his ills as if that's all he were:
Just a bundle of woes on two legs and a stick,
Never seeing the good (and not even quite sick).
So that's how things went—

That is, till *one* day...

When finally one morning a strange thing occurred
When, I think, *God Himself* had finally heard
Quite enough of the quibbles of Blaine, Baxter Q.,
And decided to patch Baxter up, good as new.

True, it's only my guess. It's just what I think.
But I think that those woes of his rose such a stink
That Good God Almighty looked down from His cloud
And said *"Stop your grumbling, for crying out loud!"*
Then God rolled up His big floppy sleeves and He vowed:

"I'll fix Baxter's ailments, each last little bit,
So that maybe—just *maybe*—his complaining will quit!"

That must be what happened, that morn' as Bax snoozed...

...'Cause, when he woke up—Baxter got the *good news!*
God had undid the knots in his *knotty insides,*
And Bax had no more *sniffles,* or *hiccups,* or *hives,*
And his *bones* didn't ache, nor his *elbows* or *thighs,*
And it no longer hurt when he'd *bat-bat* his eyes,
And his *pimple* cleared up like the sky after rain,

And the *bug* fled his head
And the *buzz* left his brain,
And his *dizzy spells* stopped,
And his *too-soggy tears*
Melted the *wax* which had clogged up his ears,
And that wax moistened up
Baxter's creamy-soft skin,
And filled in the *dimple*
That dimpled his chin,
And his *cowlick* lay down
Like a freshly mowed lawn,
And his *too-flecky freckles* and *neck-crick* were gone,
And that *scratchy old frog*
Hopped clean out of his chest,
And his *teeth* shone like pearls
From the east to the west,
And he had no more reason
To lie in his bed,
'Cause his *pants* fit just fine
When he stood on his head,
And it hurt not a bit
When he'd *squat* on one knee,
And his car kept its *oil*
And his cat lost that *flea*...

And Bax felt *extra* good, not the least little pain,
Not even a *twitch'l* of which to complain,
God had cured every last little *stress'l* and *strain*—
Yes, he felt so darn chipper, so *diff'rent* inside,
Couldn't *bellyache, grumble,* or *gripe* if he tried,
And was so completely, so *neatly* tongue-tied...

...That Baxter Q. Blaine simply rolled up and died.

AN OPEN BOOK
*(you are a story
written by you)*

I shan't compose a sonnet
'Cuz, doggonnit, I can't rhyme.
And I'll never write a novel
'Cuz, my word, there isn't time.
I've no head for spinning lyrics
To the jingles on TV.
And how to weave a thriller
Is a mystery to me.
I couldn't pen a valentine
To lay my feelings bare.
If I tried to write a sermon,
Lord, I wouldn't have a prayer.
I cannot limn a limerick.
I could not scribe a speech.
Odes and essays are beyond me.
Epic tales are out of reach.
Yet every day, I fill a page
With drama, jest and strife
As I write another chapter
In this story called *My Life.*

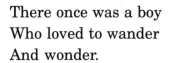

LOVE POEM
(you are what you love)

There once was a boy
Who loved to wander
And wonder.

He'd explore every cave
And poke 'round every grave
And turn each new rock
To look under.
He loved diggin' holes
And he loved climbin' trees,
And settin' the dandelions loose
On the breeze...

But he loved still better
To sit very still
And ponder the whys
And the reasons,
So he set to his wonderin'
And his mind went to wanderin'
As the leaves marked the passing
Of seasons.

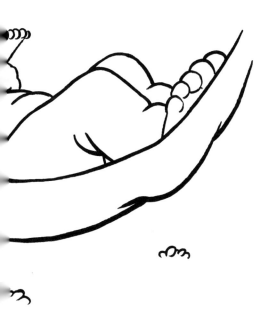

And now this old man
Doesn't dig any holes
Or climb trees
Or turn rocks anymore,
He just lies in his bed
And explores in his head
And writes silly love poems
And snores.

WHAT GETS MY GOAT
(you are what you hate)

You know what really
Pops my cork?
What frosts my mug and
Steams my shorts?
You know what makes me
Soooo irate?

All the awful, dreadful,
People who *hate!*
So I'm marking 'em down
Then I'm wiping my slate,
From the mumbliest grumbler
To the loudest ingrate:

I'll dump all the grumpies,
The grouchies and drearies.
I'll get cross with the crabbies.
I'll deplore the uncheeries.
I'll be peeved at the peevish.
I'll despise the de-spiteful.
I'll detest every human not *ultra*-delightful.
And much as I hate to,
I'm not stopping there—
I'll make sure our *four-legged* friends
Get spited their share:
I'll hate dogs who hate cats,
And cats who hate mice,
And the mice for their hatred
Of their wee hateful lice...

And I won't stomach kids
Who hate peas on their plate,
Nor friends who leave early
Or planes that leave late...

And I'll hate—

...What?

Whaddya mean, you're *hating* my poem!?
Hey don't turn the page!
Hey, where are you goin'!?

HEY!...

(I hate when that happens.)

MY VERY OWN NATION
(you are your imagine'nation)

My nation isn't Greece or Bali.
Don't live in Spain.
Not Minsk 'ner Mali.
Not Turkey, Togo, Tonga too.
Not far Qatar, nor Tuvalu.
My nation's not the U.S.A.
Or East Rangoon or Bimbombay.
Don't look for me in the village square.
Don't waste your time. Won't find me there.
I don't dwell in some distant land.
Or a buggy jungle. Or a world of sand.
I travel far and ramble wide.
(Don't go nowhere, just sit inside.)
Don't need no train, nor a motorsickle.
Won't cost a dime. Not near a nickel.
Don't spin your globe. Ain't on no maps.

I just screw on my thinkin' cap
And build a kingdom in my head
Outta magic beans and gingerbread.
When I'm in need of fascination,
Get a hunger for some inspire'ation,
I start an inner explore'ation
To conquer my Imagine'Nation:

I can saddle up my old nag Nellie.
I can pluck the button from an ogre's belly.
I can catch Niagra when it Falls,
Got a ready head when adventure calls.
I can shatter space. Demolish time.
I can squeeze an orange 'til it dribbles rhyme.
Can't get too gloomy. Not too bored,
When I'm battlin' off a beastly hoard.
I can win a tussle with a lunging leopard.
I can swallow fire—like it salt and pepper'd.
I can conjure up enchanted spells,
Toss a wicked witch down a wishin' well.
I can stretch tall as ten men combined
Or shrink down small as a gnat's behind.
When life is long, when my day is dull,
Let a monkey loose inside my skull.
Spacemen. Cowpokes. Buccaneers.
Got a rowdy crowd between my ears.

I can't move out. You can't move in.
Only room for one inside my skin.
Say you need a brain vacation?
Got a noggin full of constern'ation?
Don't be a lump, just vegetatin'—
Go visit your Imagine'Nation.

WHEN YOUR PICKLE'S IN A PINCH
(you are the challenges you face)

When your pickle's in a pinch
When you're battling every inch
When you're coming to the clinch
When it's certain it's a cinch
A sinch'uation you can't win—
Don't give in!

When your undie's in a bundle
And your courage takes a tumble
Then your tummy gives a grumble
'Cause there's nothing left but humble
Humble pie to eat or die—
That's when you try!

When you'd rather fight than switch
But you're down and in the ditch
So low, you make the poor look rich,
Kid, when it's too hot in the kitch
In the kitchen from the heat—
Don't be beat!

When you're weary as a lizard
'Cause a buzzard's got your gizzard
And no magic wand or wizard
Could disappear the blizzard
Of woe that's come a'blowin'—
Keep a'goin'!

When your fiddle can't be fit
When your brow's too beat to knit
When you've caboodled your last kit
When it's grim as it can git—
...Hey, maybe it's time to quit.
(Who said that?)

ANTHONY GENE

(you are what you dream #3:
careful what you dream!)

Mom told Anthony Gene,
"You are what you dream!"
So Anthony Gene
Dreamt of peaches and cream
And never was heard from again,
While Gene's brother Pat
(Less thin now than fat)
Woke up with a peach-eating grin.

THE SPECTACLE STORE
(you are how you choose to see things)

"Grandma, why is it," I asked (being nosy),
"That Grams are so cheery? So sunny and rosy?"
And what my Grams told me, I'd not heard before,
'Bout a shop 'round the corner, called the Spectacle Store.

"You see these old specs?" Grandma said with a wink,
And she showed me her glasses, all rosy and pink.
"These make my world brighter—helps more than you'd think.
Now scoot, off to bed," and I slept in a blink.

Later that night, long after bedtime,
'Jammie pockets jam-packed full of nickels and dimes,
I snuck out, 'round the corner, in search of the place,
To buy me some glasses to hang on my face.

And there, in an alley, as big as could be,
Stood a tiny wee store, much too small to hold me.
Or at least so it seemed till I stepped through the door
Of that shop, which I'm sure never stood there before.

"A good evening Young Miss, on this fine purple night,"
Said the hairless shopkeep through a beard blizzard-white.
"Have you come to buy sweets? Parakeets? Trundle beds?"
"We see none of those," said the eyes in my head.

"Well you might if you looked in a trundle bed store.
As for me I sell specs—I've got glasses galore!"
And yes, so he did, from the roof to the floor,
More pairs of eyeglasses than a nose ever wore.

"I see. But you see, Sir," I spoke up and said,
"My Grams wears eyeglasses that cheer up her head
'Cause the glass of her lens is the color of rose,
So please, might I purchase a small pair of those?"

The shopkeep seemed careful, his answer to choose.
He consulted a tomcat, who roused from a snooze
A sleepy old basset of age antiquated—
The hound woofed his piece, then the shopkeep translated:

"'Course, rose-colored glasses are favored, it's true,
For Grandmas and Grandpas with grandkids like you.
'Cause it helps," said the man, "keep their energy up,
Like the smile an old dog wears, when it plays with a pup."

"But you," said the shopkeep, now leaning in close,
"Don't look—'least to me—all too glum or morose.
There's a *worldful* of colors of glass to propose,
And Lass, 'lest you doubt me, have a look on *my* nose."

That's when I noticed the old fellow wore
Not *one* pair of specs, but two or three—maybe four—
Piled one 'top another, in a colorful jumble.
"How do you see at *all?*" was all I could mumble.

"Oh I see very well, and I see very clearly!
For you see," said the man, "on my walls there are nearly
Three thousand, five hundred and one frames of mind!
Every possible outlook! Every color and kind!

"I've got bright sunny specs! I've got specs with the blues!
I've got specs green with envy! I've got angry red hues!
Every spec in the spectrum, from *spec A* to *spec Z!*
The question is, Miss—what might *your* outlook be?"

What was my *outlook?* What a question to ask!
But he asked with such manners, I sensed that they masked
Some unspoken truth, and his words proved me right:
"See, this first pair *I'm* wearing are my specs of *polite.*"

As he showed me the shades on the tip of his schnoz
I could feel no more muddled had I landed in Oz.
"*Polite*-colored glasses? But how can that *be?*"
Then he nicely—most *politely*—explained it to me.

"Do you sometimes neglect to smile and say *please?*
Get your toes in the soup? Not *gesundheit* a sneeze?
It's all in your outlook!" said the old man. "You ought
Try my good-mannered specs—they're *polite* to a fault!"

And before I could speak, he plunked on my beak
A pair just like his, so I gave them a peek,
And... *"Gracious! My goodness! How extr'ordinary!
Kind sir, please thank you! Why, thank you so very!"*

"Thank *you*," said the man. "No, thank *you*," answered I.
And we thanked back and forth till our *thankers* ran dry:
*"Oh, bless you!" "You're welcome!" "You're entirely too kind!"
"You're kinder times three!"* and I'd 'bout lost my mind...

Till we thankfully stopped when that glass-nabbing cat
Snatched off those *polite* specs. "Oops. Sorry 'bout that,"
Said the shopkeep, "No, *manners* is not what you're needing.
Nor glasses for *humble,* nor *pouting* or *pleading*...

"...Nor *fine-printy reading,*" mused the man as he wandered
O'er his wall full of glass. "What's the right shade," he pondered,
"For a shy youthful lass?" Then he reached way up high
And he picked out a fresh pair. "Care to give these a try?"

"I s-s'pose so," I stammered, so timid at first
As I put on those new specs, expecting the worst.
They were *plum*-ishy tinted, big and round, not too thick—
What would I find inside them? Some weird eyebally trick?

But it all became clear from the moment I gazed
Through those *plumperky* glasses—my eyes were amazed!
"Of course! Now I see it," I bubbled with glee,
"Why, life's *plumb* fantastic! Wouldja wrap these for me!"

The shopkeep just smiled as I gushed to no end—
"I'll buy all my spec's here! I'll bring every friend!
By the way," I exclaimed like a loon gone bombastic,
"What's this color, good Sir?" He said: *"Enthusiastic!"*

"Enthused-colored glasses? Sounds ever so nifty!
Wrap up a boxful! I'll take about fifty!"
I swear, I'd have bought every pair in the place
Had the shopkeep not plucked those specs *plumb*-off my face.

"My, that was fun," blushed my old bashful self
As he set those *enthusers* back safe on the shelf.
"But I'd tie poor old Grams in an old granny-knot
If I wore those specs home—what else have you got?"

"What else have I got! Child what could I lack?
There's every shade made," he said, "there on that rack.
Why, even to list them without passing out
I'd need *long-winded* specs on the end of my snout!"

So the tabbycat reached up and knocked down a pair
Of those breezy *long-wind'ers*, to give him some air,
And the shopkeep proceeded to show me the works
As I checked out each pair and observed all their quirks.

I tried lenses of *spunky*. I wore blinkers of *cheery*.
I inspected specs *gloomy*, specs *dismal* and *dreary*.
I eyed glasses of *giggly* and peepers for *weepers*,
Horn-rims for night-owls and shades for *late-sleepers*.

I saw specs of *adventuresome, dauntless* and *bold*
(And a *wet-noodle* pair of *just-do-as-you're-told*).
"Are your glasses *half-empty?* Is life looking dull?
Toss them out!" cried the shopkeep. "Buy a pair that's *half-full!*"

I wore *royal blue* spectacles, regal and proud—
The tabby turned sheepish! The basset was cowed!
There were glasses of *kindly*, and glasses of *malice*,
And *Looking-Glass* glasses for lasses named Alice...

...*Goggles* for ogglers, *spyglasses* for spies,
Late-bloomer 'zoomers and *sights for sore eyes*,
Maniacal monocles and *made-in-the-shades*,
And *spectacle* specs of *I-love-a-parade*...

...Every dang disposition that a mind's eye might see—
Every spec in the spectrum, from *spec A* to *spec Z!*
So many glasses! How would I ever find
The right shade for *me*, and *my* frame of mind?

But just as I readied to clutch at *despair*—
Some wee, smallish spectacles tumbled into my hair
From the spot where they'd rested, up, up near the ceiling
Till an inchworm inched by, and 'd sent those specs reeling...

...And I saw, when I gave that wee pair a *look-see,*
That *this*—yes *indeedie!*—was the right look for me!
And I gaped and I gawked till my eyelids grew wearied
Then I wore out the shopkeep with the questions I queried:

"How do I buy these specs? What do they cost?
Who do I call if they're broken or lost?
Are they easily scratched? Will they fog if I sneeze?
Just how does one care for a pair such as these?"

And I offered three nickels, five dimes and a penny
Plus the lint in my pocket, but he wouldn't take any.
"Oh no," said the shopkeep, "you don't have to pay,
You just have to *want* to see things that way.

"They won't pinch your nose, or fall off your head,
See, these glasses are worn on the *inside* instead.
And a scratch? Disappears with each morning's sunrise
When you wipe all the sleepydust clear from your eyes."

And with that, the old man gave a wave of his hand
And those specs filled with stars, and my eyes filled with sand,
And quick as two blinks, I was back in my room
With the sun creeping up like a rose all abloom...

And I thought, for a wink, I must have been dreaming,
At least to my mind that's the way it was seeming
Till I polished my peepers and gave them a gander
And my room—and the world—looked oh so much grander...

...And *greener!* And *oranger!* And *bluer* than *blue!*
And *purpler,* and *pinker!* And, yes, *rosier* too!
Every color and hue more alive than before,
Just as I'd seen—through those specs—in that store!

It was wondrous and weird! It was cool and chaotic!
Things looked fresh and familiar, yet strange and exotic!
Both *ants-in-my-pantsy* and calm as a clam,
Audacious and spacious, all *green eggs and ham*...

...The *light* full of *dark,* and the *dark* turning *sunny,*
The *hot* running *cold,* and the *grim* filled with *funny,*
Every shade of emotion, every mindset and mood
Was mine for the taking in each vista I viewed...

...And I knew! I now owned the most special specs made!
Eyeglasses of *rainbow*—for they show every shade
That life has to offer and a mind's eye might see—
Every spec in the spectrum, from *spec A* to *spec Z.*

Part 4

You Are How The World Sees You
(the whole world is looking at *me?*)

A TWENTY-TON TOAD
(are you the worst thing you ever did?
seems like it, sometimes)

You'll have to forgive me, I'm busy right now
    Trying to unteeter my totter,
        I stuck myself up here—I won't say just how—
            When I did something worse than I ought'r...

All the good deeds I've done are piled high with me
    On the up-side of this teetie-tottie,
        While down over there is one ugly green deed
            That wasn't so nice (it was naughty!)...

See, a dozen kind acts make a light, airy load
    So you get quite a few to the pound,
        But that bad deed I did, that's a 20-ton toad
            And it seesaw'd me clean off the ground...

'Cause it's not like a swing, winging hither and yon
    To bring you right back where you started,
        Or a merry-go-round, where if you hang on,
            You'll end up at the spot you departed...

Nope, a 20-ton toad is real hard to undo,
    It's all people see or remember,
        So let's call this warning my good deed to you—
            'Cause I want to get down by December!

THE BIG DESK
(you are what you own?)

"He must be an important man,"
  Said Number One to Two.
"Oh is that so?" said Two to One,
  "Whatever did he do?"

"Well, I'm not sure," replied the One,
  "I've never met him face-to-face,
But in his office is a *desk*
  That's the largest in the place."

"Oh I see," said Number Two.
  With new respect he went his way,
And when he met with Number Three,
  Two had this to say:

"He is a man of some renown,
  His talents multiformous."
"What's he done?" asked Number Three.
  Said Two, "His desk's enormous!"

"A man of power, certainly,"
  So Three to Four surmised.
"A desk so grand—a nobleman!
  I shouldn't be surprised."

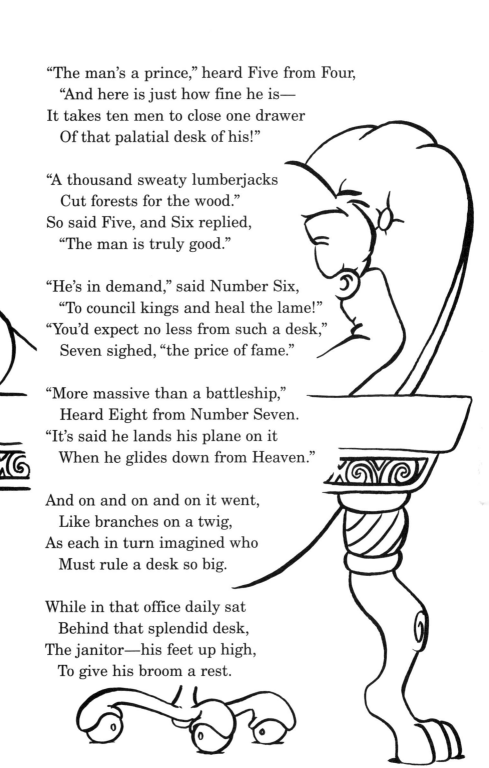

"The man's a prince," heard Five from Four,
  "And here is just how fine he is—
It takes ten men to close one drawer
  Of that palatial desk of his!"

"A thousand sweaty lumberjacks
  Cut forests for the wood."
So said Five, and Six replied,
  "The man is truly good."

"He's in demand," said Number Six,
  "To council kings and heal the lame!"
"You'd expect no less from such a desk,"
  Seven sighed, "the price of fame."

"More massive than a battleship,"
  Heard Eight from Number Seven.
"It's said he lands his plane on it
  When he glides down from Heaven."

And on and on and on it went,
  Like branches on a twig,
As each in turn imagined who
  Must rule a desk so big.

While in that office daily sat
  Behind that splendid desk,
The janitor—his feet up high,
  To give his broom a rest.

ROSE IS A ROSE

(is your name to blame?)

There once was a rose named *Rose,*
But that wasn't the name she'da chose.
"I'd prefer something frilly
Like *Petunia* or *Lily,*"
Sighed the sumptuous but silly red Rose.

A bee (named Honey) buzzed, "Rose,
Your name needs no ribbons and bows!
Sweet Rose, don't go loco,
A *Rose* ain't *Rococo*—
Why dress up a diamond in clothes?"

"I'm humdrum and dull," dithered Rose,
"And my name is to blame. Just suppose
What great thoughts I'd be thinkin'
Were I *Plato* or *Lincoln*—
Lord, I wish I wern't plain stinkin' Rose!"

A boulder (named Rock) rumbled, "Rose,
Your name's not your fame, Heaven knows!
It's that red, rosy blush
On your petals so plush,
Rose, you'd turn hearts to mush,
Every poet would gush,
(Even *I'd* get a crush)
If you'd only just shush
And not wish what you wush, stupid Rose!"

"But my name is too modest," moaned Rose.
"Lordy, grant me the wish I propose!
I would be so much grander as *Rozalakazander*,
Or stylish and swoony
As *Pinkie Marooney*
Or *Scarlotta Perfoomy*
Or *Crimzin D. Bloomie*
But *Rose?* That won't do me!
Don't like it? So *Sue* me!
But forget that you knew me as *Rose!*"

Then a Voice from above thundered, "ROSE!
You are *ROSE* from your tips to your toes!
You're my elegant, glamorous
Achingly amorous, rugged, uprootable
Pin-on-a-suit'able, fiery and florid
So-haughty-you're-horrid, passionate, petulant
Odor-from-Heaven-scent, vexing vermilion
One-flower-in-a-billion, rosy-red-nursery-rhyme
Please-be-my-valentine, classy but corny-ish
Ever-so-thorny-ish, wildly splendiforous
Stunningly snifforous, showy and striking
(And quite-to-my-liking)
Ruby red ravishing ROSE!

"But, if you insist..."

Then that flower, that formerly *Rose,*
Got her wish, and a *new* name was chose...
And that's why, my darlin',
This gift from my garden
Is a blushing red bouquet of *Joes!*

FUR THAT CAN PURR
(you are what you wear?)

If you are what you wear
(So I'm told, so I've read)
I think I'll wear kittens on top of my head.
I prefer to wear fur that can purr
And catch mice,
Plus a long kitty tail for a tie would look nice.

I find that a python works best for a belt,
It's the snuggliest belt that my belly has felt
(Though my gerbil-socks tend to get nervous),
And 'gator galoshes
That *snap* at the toe
Clear the sidewalks and give years of service.

To ward off a chill (or a squirrel better still)
A tail-wagging Afghan looks smashin',
But the Belle of the Ball
In a sweater or shawl
Of *giraffe*-ghan's the *height* of high fashion.

Octopus underwear never falls down,
It holds all your odds and your ends in.
(What's that? Got the sense
That your undies are jugglin'?
Rent a tent, give a show! Call your friends in!)

Picnics go perfect with anteater pants.
Mole-mittens work well, if you give 'em a chance.
A porcupine shirt. A butterfly vest.
A dungbeetle brooch crawlin' over my chest.
I know it's been said. I've tried it, it's true—
If you are what you wear...

...I must be a *zoo!*

104

JENNIFER FOUR
(you are your numbers)

May I recount a sad-but-true yarn,
The demise of Miss Jennifer Four—
A delightful young lady of numberless charm
Who lived over a Five & Ten store?

Now our Miss Four, though a mere One & Twenty,
Like most everyone else, carried numbers aplenty
Up there in her head like a big ball of strings,
Quite a number of numbers, for a number of things:

There were digits, of course, in her address and Zip,
And those dollars she owed on her *charge 'em card* slip,
Her best bowling score, some old lock combinations,
Plus wages and taxes and churchly donations,
Countless numbers to ring up her friends and relations,
The digity dials to her radio stations,
Her *size-Thirteen* sneakers, her heart-thumping rate,
And the calorie count of each pretzel she ate.

So it figures, one day, when her number-strings tangled
Up there in her head, that a number got mangled
And she wrote down a figure, and a digit got dangled
On a form she was filling for a job that she'd wrangled.

Such an innocent error. A slipup so slight.
A mistake so minor as anyone might.
So totally teensy and trifling...*except*—

...It woke a *computer* that was better left slept.

See, our numbers can count for a lot nowadays,
And a goof gums things up in a number of ways,
'Cause those numbers add up—they tally who's who—
And a misnumbered number, that simply won't do.

Well, the next thing you know, that computer it pounced
On that slightly wrong figure, and that form it got bounced,
And that big number-cruncher took off number-smashin'
And chomped Jenny Four in a most *un*friendly fashion:

It started off slow, *discombobbling* her clocks,
Gobbling up half their numbers, so they'd *tick*—but no *tocks*.
It *flumjumbled* the channels on her cable TV
And set her VCR back to One Million BC.
It *scrumbled* her speed-dial, and unzipped her Zip...

Then it called up her data, and that mean microchip
Gave her *SSN number* to a parrot named Lenny,
And drained her piggy bank dry, sucked in every last penny
Of her *digital dough,* through the wires of the Net,
Sent it off to Las Vegas, where it made a big bet
And blew her last *cyberbuck* on a spin of roulette...

...But if you think that's bad, you ain't heard *nuthin'* yet.

That computer reached out with its tentacle'd reach,
Snorfled in Jenny's numbers like some big number-leach,
Then it filled in the loops of her *Eights* and her *Sixes,*
Tossed her *Two's* in a bucket of *Two-Eating Grixes,*
Poked her *Nines* in the *'i'* and bit off their heads,
Made her *Ones* feel all lonely in their little-one beds,
And Oh! her plump *Zero's* it popped like a bubble
Till nothing was left but some small, O-shaped rubble.
Then it *scruffled* her *Sevens,* and *flustered* her *Fives,*
And *thrashed* her poor *Threes* near an inch of their lives.
And it *flummoxed* her *Fours* till they were flat *flabbergasty,*
But it was just warming up, folks...

...'Cause *next* it got *nasty.*

That computer...

...Subtracted Jenn's *weight* from her telephone number,
Divided her *height* by her hours of slumber,
Calculated her *birthdate* in board-feet of lumber
Multiplied by the *cube root* of a moldy cucumber.
Then it minus'd a *Nine* for each nose on her face,
Removed *Thirteen* more for each planet in space,
Erased *all* her numbers, with nary a trace...

...And zero'd Jennifer out to the *Thirty-Third* place.

Yes, it *scrunched* every digit, both even and odd,
Swept up the remainder and e-mailed it to God.
And to this very day, when you write down a *Four,*
You will hear just a hint of an *oops*—

...And no more.

Now the moral of this tale, what's it all add up to?
Only this: mind your numbers, 'cause it's certainly true
That even if *numbers* don't quite = *you*
There's some dumb computer that figures they do.

CINDYLOU KNOX HAS
ESCAPED FROM HER BOX!
(you are how others see you—unless...)

WARNING!

Cindylou Knox has escaped from her box!
The one with the pretty pink label that read:

LIST OF INGREDA'MINTS:

"One smallish girl with dark curly tresses..."
    (So she couldn't like lizards or bullfrogs, our guess is.
    I tell you what, let's stick her in dresses!)
"Awfully young, just 10 years old..."
    (Only knows what she's been told.)
"Lives way down on Blinker Street..."
    (Isn't that where all the bad kids meet?
    I'm sure I heard that once.)
"Got a C on her 'rithmetic test..."
    (Poor Cindylou, must be slower than the rest.)
"Legs are short, not so tall...."
    (Can't be much good at volleyball.)
"Puts ketchup on her lima beans..."
    (*Pssst!* We all know what that means!)
"Lately seen doing such-and-such..."
    (And we don't like *that* very much!)
"Not too fat, not too thin..."
    (Just fit that box we put her in!)

...Be on the lookout!
Cindylou Knox squeezed out of that box!
She ripped up the label and tossed it away
And she ran off skipping and laughing to play
Went off on her own, and found her own way
And now we don't know at all what to say...

...There's just no telling what Cindylou might do,
Now that she's escaped from her box!

WORD BALLOONS
(you are what you say)

Did you ever say something you meant not to say?
Some tumble of words that spilled out the wrong way
And you wished you had zipped up your loose lips instead
Of letting those *word balloons* loose from your head?

> ...yes those
> float-away get-away,
> hey-they-went-thataway,
> oops-sorry-sent-astray,
> not-what-I-meant-to-say,
> bombs-away blown-away,
> slip-away   stowaway,
> castaway throwaway,
> never-quite-go-
> away word
> balloo-
> o..
> o..
> n..
> s..

Maybe you started some nice juicy rumors
("Hey, who kissed Aunt Sally last night in her bloomers?")
Or promised a promise—gave your word like a boast—
And now that word haunts you, like a wispy word-ghost.
Or maybe you tattled, or fibbled a fib.
Or hurt a friend's feelings with your chatter so glib.
Or whispered a secret you swore that you'd keep.
Or spoke up in anger. Or talked in your sleep.

And you never imagined how *far* words could stray.
So you give it a think and your brain says "Okay,
I'll just take those words back, 'cause
They're making me queasy..."

...Well good luck, *blabberpuss,* 'cause it isn't that easy!

Once those slip'ry word bubbles sneak out of your mouth,
They're *getaway gone,* headed North, East, and South
And every which way that the four winds are wailing,
Till every ear's heard your dark word-clouds come sailing
Like runaway rockets, or trains off the track—
When those word-bombs start falling
Who knows where they'll smack.
Like a smelly old sock, the darn stink blows sky-high,
And you, *you're* the stinker! *You* let those words fly!

       ...those darn
     chase'em-and-bop'em,
    grab-a-bucket-and-mop'em,
   lend-an-ear-and-eavesdrop-
  'em, cook-some-flapjacks-and-
flop'em, get-a-sponge-out-and-
sop'em, call-the-pigs-in-and-
  slop'em, just-no-way-to-
    stop'em word
    balloo..
   o..
   o..
   n..
   s..

Ever try to deflate a huge word-blimpy mess?
Only one way to burst it—stand and shout *"I confess!*
I caused the commotion you're hearing about
When my big mouth flopped open
And those word-poops popped out!"

'Course, word balloons come with their owner's name on 'em
(For others to read, when they stumble upon 'em),
So why *'fess up* aloud, if folks know anyway?
'Cause to hear people tell it, you *are* what you *say.*

BRUCE EMERSON & MILDRED MAE

*(you are your years—
or maybe not)*

Bruce Emerson asked Mildred Mae
As they rocked their chairs one day,
"Mildred, may we dance and play?"
"We may not," said Mildred Mae.

Said Mildred Mae, "How can we dance?
With your bowed legs? My baggy pants?
At such an age, you'd find romance?
Sorry, Brucie—not a chance."

Bruce Emerson told Mildred Mae,
"Mildred, come! Let's run away!
We'll taste the ocean's misty spray
And dip our skinnys in the bay."

Said Mildred Mae to naughty Bruce,
"The sea's too salty. Drink your juice.
You want to feel the ocean lapping?
Bruce Emerson, you should be napping!"

"Please Mildred," said Bruce Emerson,
"Let's touch the sand and warming sun.
(You know, I'm fond of older women)
Mildred Mae, won't you come swimmin'?"

Said Mildred, "Bruce, you wrinkled prune!
We'd sunburn on those sandy dunes!
(And silly boy, don't be a dunce—
I'm only older by two months!)"

Said Bruce, "We're frail and toothless, true,
But Mildred Mae, if I hold you
Then we can dance our whole all lifelong—
Our knees are weak, but love is strong..."

...Then on that bright and shiny day,
Bruce Emerson and Mildred Mae
Cast all their earthly cares away
And raced off down the sand, to play.

TERRY AND THE TRUCKER
(are you sugar & spice
or puppydog tails?)

Hardtop Harry was a terror
Like no highway'd ever seen.
Harr' was cuss'ed, rough 'n tumble.
Harr' was terrible and mean.
Haulin' hogs from Heck to Hannibal
And harps to Harpers Ferry—
T'wern't no bigger, badder trucker
Ever towed a load than Harry.

Now, Sweet Terry waited tables
Down at Mabel's Dingy Diner.
("Though Our Burger's Indigestible,
The Fries Ain't Any Finer!")
Every semi steered for Mabel's
Out on Highway 101...
("Feeding Lonely Souls and Truckers
Home and Heartache on a Bun!")

Eighteen hours of dusty driving.
Eighteen days behind the wheel.
Hardtop Harry's eighteen wheeler
Stopped at Mabel's for a meal.
But Harry hadn't picked a seat
Or even took a bite,
Before that testy trucker
Picked a fellow there to fight.

When Pitstop Pete asked Harry,
"Hardtop, pass the ketchup, please?"
Harry poked Pete in the kisser!
Harry knocked him in the knees!
T'wern't no rhyme or reason to it,
Just rude Harry havin' fun—
Gettin' rowdy and unruly
Out on Highway 101.

And quick as greasy lightning
Men were bleedin' on the floors—
Harry flung 'em through the windows!
Harry heaved 'em out the doors!
While away off in a corner
Hid beneath a tippy table,
Terry watched the battle raging
Lyin' safe with poor old Mabel...

"Who's that wild and wicked trucker?"
Terry asked of Mabel, tremblin'.
Mabel said, "That's no-good Harry,
Got my diner disassemblin'."
Now, Terry was a gentle soul
With a heart as good as golden,
But a single look was all it took—
Terry's tender heart was stolen.

Old Mabel's old, but Mabel's wise,
She saw the fire in Terry's eyes.
"Now Hon'," said Mab', "please realize
That thorn's no rose in drab disguise.
That Hardtop Harry's one bad seed.
That trucker's trouble, guaranteed.
Just rambles on—a tumbleweed—
A sort like that's not what *you* need."

But Terry'd barely heard a word
Of what old Mabel said
'Fore Harry picked their tippy table
To smack on Pitstop's head.
Then Harry spotted Terry,
And the moon and stars stood still.
And when Terry smiled at Harry—
One Jack had found his Jill.

Terry tamed that tusslin' trucker
Like sugar sweetens spice.
Pitstop Pete gave 'way the bride,
Old Mabel threw the rice.
Now when that truckin' twosome
Hitch up and hit the road,
A bitty baby carriage is
The load that's gettin' towed.

So ends the simple, sappy tale
Of a happy gal and guy
(Though you may have got it backwards,
If so, don't ask me why!)
When that gentle waiter Terry
Found his truckstop Juliet
In a cuss'ed, muscled *missus*
Known as Hardtop Harri...ette!

What's that? You haven't got it yet?
Let's give it one more whirl:
Sweet Terry was the *boy,* you see—
Trucker Harry was the *girl!*

Part 5

You Are Part Of Something Bigger
(you are *we*)

KATIE ATE A KATYDID
(you are your friends)

Katie ate a katydid
Then Dottie did 'cuz Katie did
Then Trina, Bruce and Bonnie did
'Cuz Kate was keen, and Kate was cool—
If Kate ate bugs, then that's the rule!
And Melvin just threw up.

The grossest, most amazing feat!
To eat an insect whole, complete!
If Katie did, it *must* be neat!
So Hector, Biff and Wendy Lou
Gulped one apiece, and Tim ate two,
And Melvin tossed his cookies.

Soon all the friends that Katie had—
Lucinda, Linda, Kit and Chad—
Were bitten by Kate's buggy fad.
Serina, not to be outdone,
Ate several purple furry ones
And Melvin lost his lunch.

Before she knew it, Kate's creation
Had spread the globe and swept the nation—
An insect-dining infestation!
Midge ate moths 'most every day,
June bugs went down April Mae,
Ann ate ants on melted cheese,
Freddy made a feast of fleas,
Lester chomped a lighting bug
And glowed until they pulled his plug,
Sue's breakfast had a billion eyes,
Nick snacked on sacks of dragonflies,
Chris ate crickets *twice* his size,
And Melvin hurled like cannon fire.

Reporters came—and TV too!—
To make a major bugaboo
Of Kate's unsavory derring-do,
Which led her friends, each single kid,
To do that deed that Katie did,
And Melvin barfed on the cameraman.

How could she be so brave and bold?
Please Kate, your story must be told!
Why did you gobble down that bug?
Then Katie blushed, and gave a shrug,
"I had to yawn," was Kate's reply,
"I opened up and –oops!– that fly
Flew in, and *that's* the reason why."

...And Melvin, who never ate a single bug,
Felt very left out.

WHAT A TANGLED WEB
(you are we)

Your little league, your team or group
Your treehouse club, your brownie troop
Your clan, your tribe, your sewing bee
Your flavor of ethnicity
Your civic pride, your marching band
Your stars and stripes, your motherland
Your happy home, your sweet kibbutz
Your hallowed ground, your tangled roots
Your aunts and uncles, second cousins
Blood relations by the dozens
Your neighborhood, your street, your block
Your litter mates, your feather'd flock
Your pack, your pod, your trusted crew
Your herd, your hive, your tea for two
Your bestest bud, your friend in need
Your shared beliefs, your common creed
Your Sunday songs in celebration
The cat that shares your isolation
Your loyal pooch, your teddy bear
The little man who isn't there
Your native tongue, your local gang
Your Brooklynese, your southern twang
Your solemn oath, your secret shake
The sweetheart on your wedding cake
Your ghosts of old ancestral lore
The guy who runs the corner store
Your village hall, your state and nation
The whole confused conglomeration
Your countless links, by choice or birth—
Are your membership on planet Earth.

PASS IT ON
(you are what you give away)

Clarisse gave Ling a hug
Then Ling gave one to Betty
She passed it on to Pasha
Who hugged his new friend Eddie
Ed shared that hug with Bree
And Bree gave one to me
So here's a hug for you...

...Who you gonna give yours to?

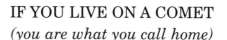

IF YOU LIVE ON A COMET
(you are what you call home)

If you live on a comet, life's a long lonely ride.
If you live in a forest, you grow moss on one side.
If home is the desert, then water's like gold.
If you move to Alaska, your toesies get cold.
Hangin' out in a cave that you share with a bear?
   Mind if I ask, why the heck you live *there?*
If you live on a mountain, your world has no *flat.*
If you live in a belfry, I'll bet you're a bat.
Are you creepy and crawly? You're under a rock.
If you're ucky toe fungus—*hey, get out of my sock!*
Wanna live in a slimy shell under the sea?
   Well, whatever you are, you're not much like me.
If home is the city, life's lived on the run.
If your heart's in the country, it beats to the sun.
When you live on a river, life floats right on by.
If God gives you wings, then you might as well fly.
Do you live like a germ in my lower intestine?
   That would explain my ga-*rumpy* digestion.
If you live in the jungle, it's eat or be eaten.
If you live way up North, rub a nose when you're greetin'.
Gonna dive in a geyser? Guess some like it hot.
If you lived in the past, in the present, you're not.
If you live in a book—book*worm* or book*lover*—
   There's one home for you, that's behind a book*cover.*

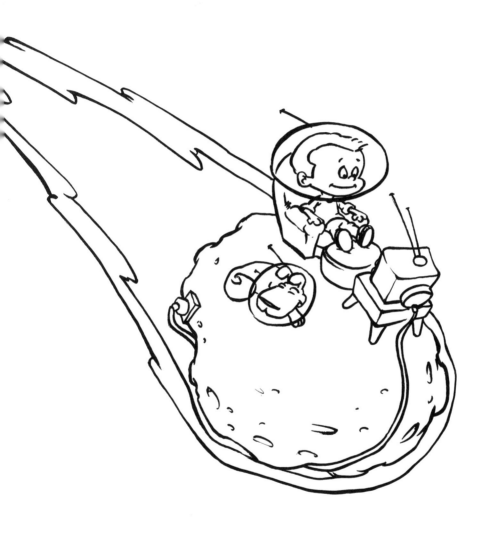

MY FAMILY
(you are your family)

My brother is a goofball.
My sister is a grinch,
She eats up all the longjohns and will not share an inch.
My mother and my father embarrass me to death.
My hamster likes to piddle.
My cat has doggie breath.
No fam'ly could be worser than this family of ours—
I'd rather be a hermit.
I'd rather live on Mars.

What's this? *Another* family just called me up to say:

"Dear Johnny, please come live with *us!*
Please, move in right away!
As Mom and Dad, we'll never scold
(We give our word, we mean it)
You'll have a bedroom all your own
(Your *new sister* has to clean it)
Your allowance is a hundred bucks
(Your *new brother's* is a penny)
We'll shower you with tons of gifts
(Both the others won't get any)
We'll feed you hot fudge sundaes
Every morning by the pool,
We'll finish all your homework—
You won't have to go to school!"

...Well pack my bags, that does sound swell!
But, golly gee, you know... my fam'ly is the worstest...

...But they'd miss me if I go.

My brother is a goofball—but I fit into his clothes,
And he taught me how to drink my milk and
Squirt it out my nose.
And my hamster *needs* to piddle on my homework after school.
And my folks are lost without me (they're so desp'rately uncool).
And my grinchy, piggy sister is too thrilled I might be leavin'...

...So I'll stay and make 'em mis'rable.
(How else can I get even?)

THE HERE AND NOW

(you are your when & where)

If I'd been born in a diff'rent *time*
And another *place* as well,
Then I would be a diff'rent *me*
With a diff'rent tale to tell:

If my daddy was a CAVEMAN
Two million years ago,
Then I would be a cave-kid
And there's lots I wouldn't know.

I'd never know who might eat who,
And brother, that's the truth,
If I lived back then and shared my den
With a hungry Saber-Tooth.

I wouldn't have much homework
'Cause there'd be no History,
And all I'd need to know is—
Can that tiger climb my tree?

I'd marvel how a ball of fire
Could ride across the sky,
And as night's stars fell over me
I could only wonder why.

I'd dread the dark, and cringe in fear
At every cracking twig,
And tremble in my cold damp cave
At a world so strange and big.

If I'd been born a SHEPHERD'S child
Six thousand years long past,
Then I would be a shepherd, too
My first day to my last.

I'd tend my flock to see that wolves
Don't gobble up my sheep,
And when I lay me down at night
I'd count 'em in my sleep.

Our little mountain valley
Is all the world I'd see,
And dinner would be mutton stew
For a shepherd kid like me.

A scruffy sheepdog, he's my pet,
Still, think how lonely we might get:
No books, no mail—no *alphabet!*
They haven't been invented yet!

Yep, food and clothes are things we'd need
And sheep would sure provide 'em,
But all that walking makes me wish—
If only I could *ride* 'em.

If I'd lived in the DAYS OF YORE
When kings still ruled their castles,
Would I be rich? Or peasant-poor?
A pauper, prince, or vassal?

Pray, what would be my lot in life?
Forsooth, it all depended—
For where ye got your *start* in life
Was likely where ye *ended*.

If my folks were upper crusty
I'd be a shiny knight,
Then I would get to horse around
Slaying dragons left and right.

But more likely I'd be lowborn
And toil in the field—
There were lots more *serfs*
   Than *squires* back then,
And by birth thy fate was sealed.

Be it God or Karma, plain dumb luck,
Or the Wisdom of the Sages,
I could only be what life chose for me
In those dark old Middle Ages.

But think of all the fun I'd had
If me mum'd had a PIRATE lad!
(Or like Anne Bonney, a pirate girl
Who wore a cap to hide her curl!)

The Spanish Main! The Seven Seas!
The sunny Isles of Caribee!
On a pirate ship, yer fancy free—
Y'can walk the plank just to take a pee!

Now I might get thirty lashes
If I didn't pull me weight, mate.
And if I tumbled in the drink
The sharks'd have me ate, mate.

But me motley scurvy pirate pals
'ud sooner wrestle with a squid
Than tell a fool landlubber where
Me chest a' bootie's hid.

And every night, we'd rock to sleep
By th' waves' perpetual motion,
As a sea of stars washed over me
In my home upon the ocean.

What if Nature'd played some tricks
And I'd grown up instead
On the far-off, future PLANET BLIX
With a turnip for a head?

I'd have my wits about me
In this alien domain,
And boss the other turnip-heads
With my big old veggie brain.

While all the other Turnip men
Were asnooze in their cocoons,
I'd hunt the dreaded Doofalo
By the light of seven moons.

Now, Turnip dudes don't move a lot
(We're rooted to the spot)—
To bag our prey, we blow our nose
And snag it with our snot.

Nine jillion skillion years from now,
Imagine if you can,
The sort of *me* that I might be
If I were Turnip Man.

But I was born in the HERE AND NOW
Which shapes my livelong days,
And makes this *me* the one you see
In oh so many ways:

No wolves are knockin' at my door,
No sharks lurk in my pool,
No dragon's dread hangs over me—
Just twelve more years of school.

I've got a million paths to choose,
They might be good or bad,
But choices that no shepherd kid
Nor caveman ever had.

I can roam the planet on the Net,
Eat a Mac in Katmandu,
Buy a robot-dog to be my pet,
And e-pop this pome to you.

Through every life runs History—
Its reasons and its rhyme,
'Cause every soul must find its *place*
In its own peculiar *time*.

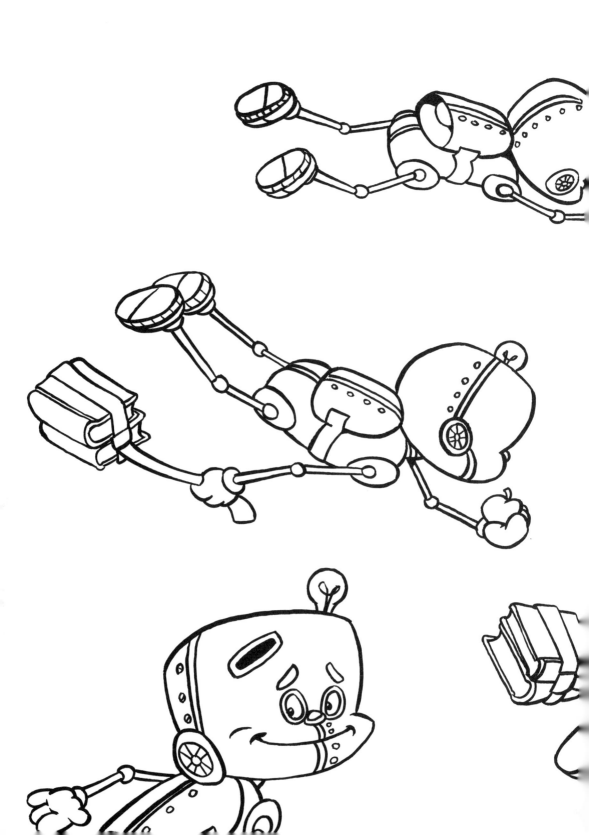

Part 6
You Will Be
(things to come...)

YESTERDAY ME, TOMORROW ME
(you are who you...
were? are? will be?)

Tomorrow isn't Yesterday.
One has gone, one's on its way.
Who I was isn't *Who I'll be*—
Why do you s'pose folks only see
That dopey little
Yester-me?

(Milk got spilled, who gets blamed?
Yesterday did it—Today was framed!)

People change, they learn and grow
Even if it doesn't show.
Forget the past and you might see
The new, improved Tomorrow Me.
If you do that, I'll do it too—
I'll keep an eye out
For Tomorrow You.

DOES EVERY SKINNY SAPLING GROW?
(you are what you might become?)

Does every skinny sapling grow to be an awesome oak?
> What a joke.

Might every movie actor someday get to play the star?
> Few ever are.

Bet every bloomin' bunnyhill grows up to be a mountain?
> That I'm doubtin'.

Think every lowly pauper takes a turn at being king?
> A most unlikely thing.

Can every caterpillar fulfill her dream to butterfly?
> Promise not to cry?

Is every seed guaranteed to grow and grow and grow?
> No and no and no.

Do every poodle use his noodle to become the *tip*-top dog?
> Go kiss a frog.

Will a rushing river wake from every sleepy stream?
> In your dreams.

S'pose every humble hamlet someday builds itself a city?
> Most stay *itty*-bitty.

Guess every guy who pushed a broom one day runs the store?
> Tell me more.

Seen every shack piggyback until it scraped the sky?
> Most don't even try.

Does every child grow to be the most that he or she can be?
> Hey, that one's up to me!

MIKEY ANGELO
DID A FINGERPAINT
(you are what you create)

Mikey Angelo did a fingerpaint
Too high to be erased.
Billy Shakespeare shined at playtime.
Izzie Duncan spun with grace.
Naughty Neil left dusty footprints
On our cheesy moonpie face.
Miz' Liz Browning scribbled sonnets.
Janie Austin tole' some tales.
Mary Shelly gave us nightmares.
Hermie Melville dreamt of whales.
Leon Ardo's ticklish paintbrush
Made poor Mona Lisa smirk.
Gali' Leo 'scoped the planets.
Icky Newton made 'em work.
Pab' Picasso broke his crayons
When he bent 'em out of shape.
Auggie Rodin had us thinkin'.
Charlie Darwin drove us ape.
'Bertie Einstein hatched a formula
That wrinkled Space and Time.
Mary Curie's gift was glowing.
Eddie Poe wrote ravin' rhyme.
Little Vincent wrassled demons
But his wheatfields were divine.

Tommy Edison left the lights on,
Turned his phonograph up loud.
Goog' Marconi played the radio.
Stevie Spielberg drew a crowd.
Mikey Jordan weaved a basket
When he jumped into the clouds.
Baby Elvis rocked and wriggled.
Scottie Joplin *plink'opated.*
Lucy bawled and we all giggled.
Ferdie Zepp'lin got inflated.
Georgie Carver cracked a goober.
Hank Houdini pulled some tricks.
Judy skipped her ruby slippers
Down Frankie Baum's bright yellow bricks.
Young John Lennon played with beetles.
Some ol' caveman played with fire.
Allie Eiffel built a spire
For the tourists to admire.
Wee Mo' Gandhi put his foot down.
Rosie Parks got on the bus.
Chuckie Shulz was full'a peanuts
And he shared the bunch with us.
Benjie Franklin bottled lightning.
Pouty Ludwig captured thunder.
Wil' and Orville sprouted feathers.
Jock's Calypso pulled us under.
Like my poem? Thank my mom, 'cuz
She made me and that's a wonder.

MISFORTUNE'S
CHILD
(you are your fate?)

The Stars drew up a map that I
  must follow on this Earth,
A plot which I could not defy,
  writ long before my birth.

Like Romeo and Julie,
  I'm a bug drawn to the flame.
If Destiny grabs hold of me
  how can I be to blame?

The Lion must chase the Lamb about,
  and Frenchmen munch their Fries.
When the Sun burns, do you shout
  "Hey Sun, apologize!"

My Nature is my Nature and
  it cannot be repealed.
My Horoscope is clear on this,
  my cursèd Fate is sealed.

No matter how I searched my soul's
  dim crevices and crookies,
There was but one path to be chose—
  I *had* to swipe those cookies!

UNFINISHED
MASTERPIECE
(you are a work in progress)

A work of art, once painted,
Is hung upon a wall,
But humans are a special art
That's never done at all.

...The End.

INDEX

THE ACHES & PAINS OF BAXTER Q. BLAINE 76
ANTHONY GENE 87

THE BIG DESK ... 100
BILLY T. COOP 30
BODYWORKS 18
BRAIN-SUCKING MONSTERS! 24
BRUCE EMERSON & MILDRED MAE ... 114

CINDYLOU KNOX HAS ESCAPED FROM HER BOX! ... 110
CREATURE OF HABITS 28

DOES EVERY SKINNY SAPLING GROW? ... 148
DUDLEY THE DREAMER 62

FINDERS KEEPERS 26
FROM WHERE I STAND 60
FUR THAT CAN PURR ... 104

A GENIUS OF FEELINGS 70

HAVE YOU MET MOLLY MEANT-TO? 65
THE HERE AND NOW ... 132
HOW TO EAT YOUR HAT 12

I CANNOT ABIDE THE CIRCUS 66
IF A PEACOCK'S ITS FEATHERS 10
IF YOU LIVE ON A COMET ... 128

JENNIFER FOUR ... 106
JIMMY McDEED 32

KATIE ATE A KATYDID ... 124

. are you what TROUBLES you?
. you are what you DREAM #3

. you are what you OWN?
. you're not a COMPUTER...are you?!
. you are your BOD'
. you are what you WATCH—so watch out!
. you are your YEARS—or maybe not

. you are how OTHERS see you—unless...
. you are a HABIT forming

. you are what you MIGHT BECOME?
. you are what you DREAM

. you are your MEMORIES—so hold on to 'em!
. you are your POINT OF VIEW
. you are what you WEAR?

. you are what you FEEL

. you are what you DO—or DON'T
. you are your WHEN & WHERE
. you are what you EAT: the food chain

. you are what you FEAR
. you are your PARTS, partly
. you are what you call HOME

. you are your NUMBERS
. you are what you READ

. you are your FRIENDS

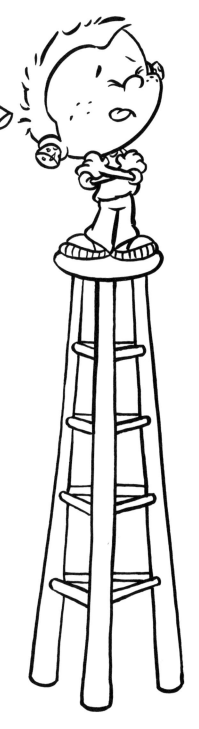

LOOK AT ME, I'M NUMBER THREE 64
LOVE POEM 81

THE MARBLE AND THE PEBBLE 16
MESSAGE IN A BOTTLE 20
MIKEY ANGELO DID A FINGERPAINT ... 150
MISFORTUNE'S CHILD ... 152
MY FAMILY ... 130
MY ON-THE-LOOSE DREAM 74
MY VERY OWN NATION 84
MYST'RIOUS ICEBERG 34

NEED'A, WANNA, GOTTA HAVE IT 72

AN OPEN BOOK 80

PASS IT ON ... 127
PLAYING GROWN-UP 68

ROSE IS A ROSE ... 102

SOMETHING CALLED BIOLOGY 13
SPECIAL DELIVERY 14
THE SPECTACLE STORE 88
SUNDAY'S CHILD 27

TERRY AND THE TRUCKER ... 118
A TWENTY-TON TOAD 98

UNFINISHED MASTERPIECE ... 154
THE UNTIED SHOELACE 40

WHAT A TANGLED WEB ... 126
WHAT GETS MY GOAT 82
WHEN YOUR PICKLE'S IN A PINCH 86
WORD BALLOONS ... 112

YESTERDAY ME, TOMORROW ME ... 146

. you are your PLACE IN LINE
. you are what you LOVE

. you are the NICKS AND SCARS you collect
. you are a LINK IN THE CHAIN
. you are what you CREATE
. you are your FATE?
. you are your FAMILY
. you are what you DREAM #2
. you are your IMAGINE'NATION
. you are what's HIDDEN INSIDE

. you are what you DESIRE

. you are a STORY written by you

. you are what you GIVE AWAY
. you are what you PRETEND to be

. is your NAME to blame?

. you are your human bean GENES
. you are exactly what your PARENTS ordered!
. you are how you CHOOSE to see things
. you are your DIS-POSITION

. are you SUGAR & SPICE or PUPPYDOG TAILS?
. are you WORST THING you ever did?

. you are a WORK IN PROGRESS
. you are your WORK & your TOOLS

. you are WE
. you are what you HATE
. you are the CHALLENGES you face
. you are what you SAY

. you are who you WERE? ARE? WILL BE?